CAMPER RECRUITMENT & RETENTION PLAYBOOK

Travis Allison

Joanna Warren Smith

ISBN: 978-1-7381323-0-0
Imprint: Independently published

You're not alone.

As a camp director, you face numerous challenges when it comes to marketing your summer camp. Time constraints, a lack of marketing expertise, and feeling overwhelmed by the sheer number of marketing channels available can make it challenging to promote your camp and fill those spots effectively.

You're passionate about providing **a life-changing summer camp experience** for kids but you're struggling to get the word out and attract new campers. Heck, you're often also struggling to get last year's campers to return. With so many marketing avenues to choose from, it's easy to feel overwhelmed and unsure of where to focus your efforts. This can lead to missed opportunities, wasted resources, and, ultimately, empty spots at your camp.

The pressure to fill your camp is mounting, and you're starting to feel the stress. You know that a successful summer camp depends on a solid marketing strategy, but **with limited time and resources, it's challenging to know where to begin**.

Camp Directors are not alone in feeling overwhelmed by marketing their camp programs. The longer you wait to address these issues, the more potential campers slip through your fingers, leaving you with empty spots and lost revenue.

For folks like you, here's the **Camper Recruitment & Retention Playbook**: your comprehensive guide to overcoming marketing challenges and filling your camp spots with ease. This workbook uses the proven systems that Joanna and I have been installing in camps for more than 20 years.

With the Camper Recruitment & Retention Playbook, you'll learn how to:

> ❯ Identify your ==target audience==* and their unique needs

> ❯ Develop a focused marketing strategy that maximizes your resources

> ❯ Leverage the most effective marketing channels for your camp

> ❯ Create compelling communications that resonate with your audience and increase registrations

> ❯ Overcome the 'overwhelm' and confidently market your summer camp

Don't let marketing hold you back any longer.

With the **Camper Recruitment & Retention Playbook**, you now have the tools and guidance to effectively promote your camp, fill those spots, and positively impact campers. But you have to do the work. So get started today and watch your camp registrations soar!

You are not alone,

Travis

Travis Allison, *Co-Founder/Co-Owner*
Go Camp Pro
travis@gocamp.pro

*Highlighted words or phrases are defined in the Playbook Dictionary on page #50.

They have 'kept me honest,' as I like to say, and they have allowed me to be even more effective with clients because **their input is direct and relevant to that year's camp experiences.**

In general, parents are realistic. They do not expect camps to be perfect; rather, they want **Directors to be vigilant, accessible, responsive, and proactive** to correct issues when they occur. And, since the pandemic, there is a newfound appreciation for camp, which is good news for our industry. Parents now have a clearer understanding of the unique environment that summer camp provides for kids and realize how essential that experience is in today's world.

It's also interesting to note that parents across the country representing diverse socio-economic backgrounds agree that there are five 'NEEDS' that are critical to a quality Parent Experience, which, if consistently delivered, will ensure that a family returns to camp year after year.

Fortunately, each of the following Camp Parent Needs or requirements are easy to implement if you do what needs to be done immediately and intentionally plan for the upcoming summer. Yes, you may have to alter 'the way you've always done it,' but that change will be based on input from parents whose children attend your camp.

TOP FIVE CAMP PARENT NEEDS
AND HOW TO BEST ADDRESS THEM

1. WEB PRESENTATION OF LEADERSHIP TEAM

Interested, new, and returning families want **EASY, direct access to your entire Leadership Team's** web page. Present staff visually and biographically in a professionally playful format that demonstrates competence and confidence. Ideally, a starburst on the website front page with a link to MEET OUR DIRECTORS would immediately take parents to the page.

When transitions in an organization happen, changes are instantaneous so that the Leadership page is <u>always</u> current.

2. OPENING DAY DETAILS

Make sure to communicate clearly with new and returning campers and parents about opening day to avoid any surprises that could turn people off. For campers, be certain to speak the language of both younger and more mature campers as appropriate. For parents, give specifics for new families and an updated presentation for returners.

Use video, coloring books, and a variety of clever presentations to **increase awareness and understanding and create a welcoming and efficient opening day**.

3. WELCOME ACKNOWLEDGEMENT

Day and resident camp parents agree that **the start of camp must be acknowledged.** In a perfect world (and none of us lives there), each resident camp family would be called to confirm for the parents that the child is settling in and all is well. The second best is that all new families are called.

If neither of those options is possible, an email/text to all parents on that first night indicating that 'everyone's unpacked, we're heading in for a spaghetti dinner, and then we're off for a big game of Capture the Flag' is essential. For day camp parents, intentional connections (check names off a list to confirm 100% coverage) with parents at drop-off or pick-up can work. **Individual phone calls or an end-of-first-day group activity email** with a comment about each child to the individual parent can be effective.

4. PROGRAM UPDATES

Too often, both day and resident camp parents talk about their child being lost in the 'big, black hole of camp.'

They don't know what the camp day looks like, they don't know what they're paying for, and, most importantly, **they don't know how to talk to their child about the camp experience**.

Consequently, when the child comes home, they ask, 'what did you do at camp?' and inevitably, the camper grunts, 'nothing'! Even though you post pictures, you owe it to the families, and it is very much to your benefit to **provide parents with 'program context'** so that they understand your program and its benefits for their camper and see reasons to returning the next season. These communications do not need to be long but regularly timed, perhaps Tuesday and Thursday @ 2 PM and, whenever possible, precise to an age group rather than generic to the entire camp.

5. CAMPER REPORT CARD

In private camps, it used to be the tradition that each parent would receive a personal letter from the Director about each child when camp concluded. It was a great retention tool, but less likely to happen now.

The concept is still very appealing to parents and can be done in a manageable way. Michelle Crocker, from YMCA Camp Cheerio, has graciously shared the following format which they have successfully used for years. Based on Focus Group responses, parents will definitely **appreciate this opportunity to know more specifics about the camp experience you provided for their children**.

CAMP CHEERIO

Camper Name: ____________________

Cabin & Session: ____________________

Senior Counselor: ____________________

Junior Counselor: ____________________

CIT: ____________________

Camper's Activities This Week
1. ____________________
2. ____________________
3. ____________________
4. ____________________
5. ____________________
6. ____________________
7. ____________________
8. ____________________

Three Words We Would Use To Describe Your Child
1. ____________________
2. ____________________
3. ____________________

Counselor Comments
____
____
____
____
____
____
____

Counselor Signature: ____________________   Date: ____________

And finally… I indicated there would be 'more later' regarding monthly communications with next summer's campers and, separately, their parents.

These two groups should be **divided into new and returning categories for maximum impact**. The information being shared and the hype to create anticipation is basically the same, but the style with which it is delivered should match each group's expectations.

If you treat all families like returners, the uninitiated often do not understand the critical details. And if you treat everyone like a newbie, then veterans are turned off.

Taking the time to craft a message for one group and then tweaking it for the other is worth the time. The 'care and nurturing' you provide as you prepare for the upcoming summer will **positively impact the subsequent season's camper retention rate**.

Commit now to provide a 'noticeably improved product' next summer.

Joanna Warren Smith, *President*
Camp Consulting Services
campconsulting@charter.net

MAXIMIZE YOUR PLAYBOOK TO INCREASE NEW ACQUISITIONS AND RETAIN MORE CAMPERS!

1) Read the introductions by Travis and Joanna and select the suggestions that resonate with you. Then set a start date and a deadline for completion.

2) Make sure to schedule a monthly meeting with your marketing team and be consistent if you're working alone.

3) The workbook is divided by months. Review the introductory comments, and if there are references that are unfamiliar, look for definitions in the **Playbook's Marketing Dictionary** (pg. #50).

4) Promote monthly to your five target networks: **Not-Yet-Enrolled Previous Campers, Not-Yet-Enrolled Previous Parents, New Acquisitions, Next Summer's Campers, and Next Summer's Parents**. Connect with Parents and Campers separately for greater impact. If feeling overwhelmed, focus on getting Not-Yet-Enrolled families to sign up - it's the easiest and most effective way to increase enrollment.

5) Nurture the relationship with next summer's campers and their parents and you strengthen your retention rate for the following year.

6) If you're considering a new technique or want a sample, check out the QR Code-linked Resource Guide for samples and communication styles (see pg #14).

7) Keep using marketing strategies that have brought back campers or attracted new ones. Try to do more promotions using techniques from the Playbook, but don't take on so much that you feel overwhelmed. **Executing one or two promotional efforts very well is better than taking on too many.**

8) Carefully track your enrollment statistics each month on the Stats pages. Knowing your current numbers compared to last year's at this time and the final count keeps you motivated. Also, track your '**Inquiry to Conversion Rate**' to see if your follow-up works.

9) Keep records of all your promotions in order by date in a Marketing Binder or computer Folder. This will give you a visual plan to refer to next year so you can repeat successful efforts and improve on less effective ones.

10) Some items in the Playbook have bonus material indicated with a superscript ^{Q} that can be found in our external Resources Guide. To access all the extra Resources marked with the ^{Q} in the Playbook, use this QR Code, and we will send you the secret link. ●——————————➤

LET'S FOCUS ON
YOUR GOALS AND OBJECTIVES

It's fine to say that you want more campers and that you'd like to increase retention, but that's not specific enough to keep you motivated for a year of recruitment efforts.

Initially, you should **determine your true capacity**. In a resident camp, that's the actual number of beds. In a day camp, capacity is often defined by the pool capacity that allows each group to swim the promised number of times.

Compare your session enrollment numbers for the past two years against session capacities to determine the areas on which to focus. You may find that early summer enrollments are softer than mid-summer numbers and then final sessions soften again. If so, consider promotions to families at private schools since they tend to end in late May/early June, so families are ready for camp earlier. And, to jazz up final sessions, consider extreme or specialty programs that might interest specific groups or returning campers.

Set achievable goals to increase enrollment by 5-7% yearly and, if you reach that goal before camp, set another achievable goal to keep yourself motivated.

Camp Professionals agree that the **minimum industry retention goal is 65%**, although many camps report 80+%. Programs consistently falling below the industry goal will have difficulty in a competitive marketplace.

With retention, the more detail, the better. A total number indicates client satisfaction or not, while **specifics help identify program/marketing issues** that can be rectified or elements that should be expanded. For instance, when you track the return rate of a specific gender and age and are confident in the marketing, and there is a major drop in the return, there is a program issue that should be solved. Or if you track the retention of bus groups at your day camp, and one group's retention is impressive, you know that the bus counselor did a stellar job and should teach their methodology during staff training.

Gather as much retention data as possible. Compare it to the last two years to get started, and then set a realistic goal to increase retention by 3-5% yearly, focusing on individual areas where erosion has been most evident. *Keep your team informed and motivated with large visuals showing enrollment progress in a prominent place so that the objective is always featured and enthusiasm is maintained.*

IN A PERFECT WORLD...

You would be ready to start the subsequent season's registration during the previous summer. And then, in September, when the sequence of the Playbook commences, you would be prepared to go full tilt to secure high retention rates and attract new acquisitions in the suggested chronological order.

But we don't live in a perfect world. And we don't want that reality to deter anyone who wants to use this Playbook.

So, you start when you start.

That's precisely the reason we've used this format that is manageable whatever month you're ready to commit. **GO FOR IT!**

Before you take a well-earned break, set up September Communications with Campers and Parents to maintain your Connections.

Many parents have told Joanna in Focus Groups how much they appreciate the 'Use Your Camp Skills & Confidence at School[Q]' communications their campers receive from camps. When they arrive, via snail mail or parent email, their kids often share great stories about their achievements at camp.

An equally impressive contact is **remembering each camper's birthday** throughout the year with some reference to the celebration tradition at camp. Kids retell the stories with such enthusiasm that it often causes parents to register for camp immediately. Please don't be tempted to send all of one month's Birthday Cards on the first of the month to make life easier. The closer to the actual date, the more impact.

As the recruitment year begins, it's critical that you **refresh ALL communications**, especially those that are targeted to returning families. Those who have been with you for multiple seasons have seen it all, and you owe it to yourself to change the presentation format, the color scheme, or the language so that returning parents and campers stay engaged. Once they become bored, they tend to seek alternative summer options!

In Section #2 (next page), there's a reference to '**Rewarding Referring Families**' and in Section #5, a reference to a '**Camper Referral System**'. The first tends to be more organic, while the second is becoming a more standard approach, which can be very productive when actively promoted.

Please don't let September slip by. Your marketing rhythm for the upcoming year depends on a strong start!

NYE* PREVIOUS CAMPERS

- **'Use Your Camp Skills & Confidence at School' via Parent Email**
- Share Changes Made Resulting from Camper Survey Input
- Connect Emotionally via Video About Returning Next Year

**NYE = Not Yet Enrolled*

NYE* PREVIOUS PARENTS

- **'Register Now to Guarantee the Session of Your Choice' Promo with or without Incentive**
- Reward and/or Thank Your Best Referring Families
- Share Changes to be Made Resulting from Parent Survey Input
- 'Re-Invest in Your Camper' Communication

NEW ACQUISITIONS

- **'What a GREAT SUMMER We Had!' Communication to all Previous/Current Inquiries, Alumni, Membership, Volunteers, Friends, and Family**
- Confirm Web Inquiry System is Simple and Working
- Revitalize Website to Show Current Camp Product
- Connect with Schools with Camper Density

NEXT SUMMER'S CAMPERS

NEW
- **'Welcome to Camp' Communication/Gift**
- 1st Installment of 'Getting to Know About Camp'

RETURNING
- **'Welcome to Camp' Communication/Gift**
- 'Use Your Camp Skills & Confidence at School' via Parent Email

NEXT SUMMER'S PARENTS

NEW
- **'Welcome to Camp' Communication**
- 1st Installment of Prepping for Camp

ALL
- **1st Dr. Deborah Gilboa or Dr. Tina Payne Bryson Article**
- Camper Referral System Explanation and Promotion

Make It Happen

Revitalize Automated Communications

Confirm Foolproof System for Tracking All Inquiries

Dissect Retention (gross/gender/age/program/session/new) to Reveal Program or Marketing Issues

Test Steps of the Registration Process

Tracking Statistics enables you to set goals, recognize trends, and proactively respond.

UC = Unique Campers / number of individual campers enrolled at a specific time - e.g., 43 campers were registered on January 20 for a total of 43 unique campers

C WEEKS = Camper Weeks / number of weeks booked at a specific time - e.g., 43 campers were registered for two weeks each on January 20 for a total of 86 camper weeks

Inquiry Conversion Rate = number of families who inquire about your programs compared to the number who register for your camp

YTD = Year to Date | **NYE** = Not Yet Enrolled

UC ENROLLED YTD	UC YTD LAST YEAR	TOTAL UC LAST YEAR

C WEEKS YTD	C WEEKS YTD LAST YEAR	TOTAL C WEEKS LAST YEAR

TOTAL NEW ENROLLED		# RETURNING %		INQUIRY/ CONVERSION RATE
YTD	Last Year	YTD	Last Year	

October is a great month to have fun with Campers.

The suggested monthly contest gets lots of kids to participate. A small camp store gift certificate for every winner costs you virtually nothing and gets everyone thinking about their return next summer. It's a win/win!

In Section #1 on the next page, the technique of **highlighting returning campers as they enroll** on the previous year's bunk/group lists provides solid insight into why campers have not yet enrolled. Both private and not-for-profit camps all over the country use this tool to guide them in their conversations with parents and it works to solve potential issues and increase retention!

A surprising number of camps report that, once a parent contacted them and they provided what was requested, the camp did nothing else to follow up with the family. This is in direct contrast to what Parents in Focus Groups report… that they want to be 'courted to the sale'. Parents realize 'camp' is a big decision and a substantial financial investment and they don't want to make a mistake.

And finally, because many camps are forced to limit capacities because they cannot hire enough staff, let's address the elephant in the room. October is the perfect time to reach out to all your families, alumni, members, and friends to **request that they share your Staff Benefits Package with a College Student or High School Senior** who would be a great role model at your camp.

This request sounds desperate in March but, at this time of the year, it's perfect with the holidays fast approaching. Remember, if we're going to help you recruit more campers, you will need more staff! Check out some sample Staff Benefits Packages.

NYE* PREVIOUS CAMPERS

- ☐ **Highlight Returning Campers on Previous Year's Bunk/Group Lists to Determine Reasons Why Others Are Not Yet Enrolled**
- ☐ Camper Contest to ID Counselor(s) in Hoodie(s) Tied Up so Only Nose Shows with ALL Winners Getting Next Summer Camp Store Gift Certificates

*NYE = Not Yet Enrolled

NYE* PREVIOUS PARENTS

- ☐ **Remind Parents of Positive Camper Outcomes & Why Kids Need Camp Today**
- ☐ Count Down to Early Bird Deadline with Email Reminders to Build Momentum PLUS Personal Phone Calls and Texts. Response By Deadline Will GUARANTEE THE SESSION OF CHOICE, which is the Ultimate Incentive

NEW ACQUISITIONS

- ☐ **Confirm Inquiry Engagement^Q Protocols and Ongoing 'Courtship to the Sale' Until Registration or Summer Starts**
- ☐ Commence Online Advertising
- ☐ Maximize Social Media Presence for Marketing Not Just Fun Pictures Being Shown

NEXT SUMMER'S CAMPERS

NEW
- ☐ **2nd Installment of 'Getting to Know About Camp'**

RETURNING
- ☐ **Camper Contest to ID Counselor(s) in Hoodie(s) Tied Up so Only Nose Shows with ALL Winners Getting Next Summer Camp Store Gift Certificates**

NEXT SUMMER'S PARENTS

NEW
- ☐ **2nd Installment of Prepping for Camp**

ALL
- ☐ **Camper Referral System Reminder**
- ☐ Counselor Benefits Package To Increase Applicant Pool
- ☐ Director Blog/Trust Building Media Post^Q

Make It Happen

Refine Marketing Systems and Other Standard Operating Procedures

Build a Monthly/Full Year Promotional Binder or Folder

Categorize, Tag, & Run Facial Recognition of Your Photos/Videos to Make Marketing Easier

Set Enrollment and Retention Goals for Next Summer

Scrutinize Retention and Enrollment Details

October STATISTICS

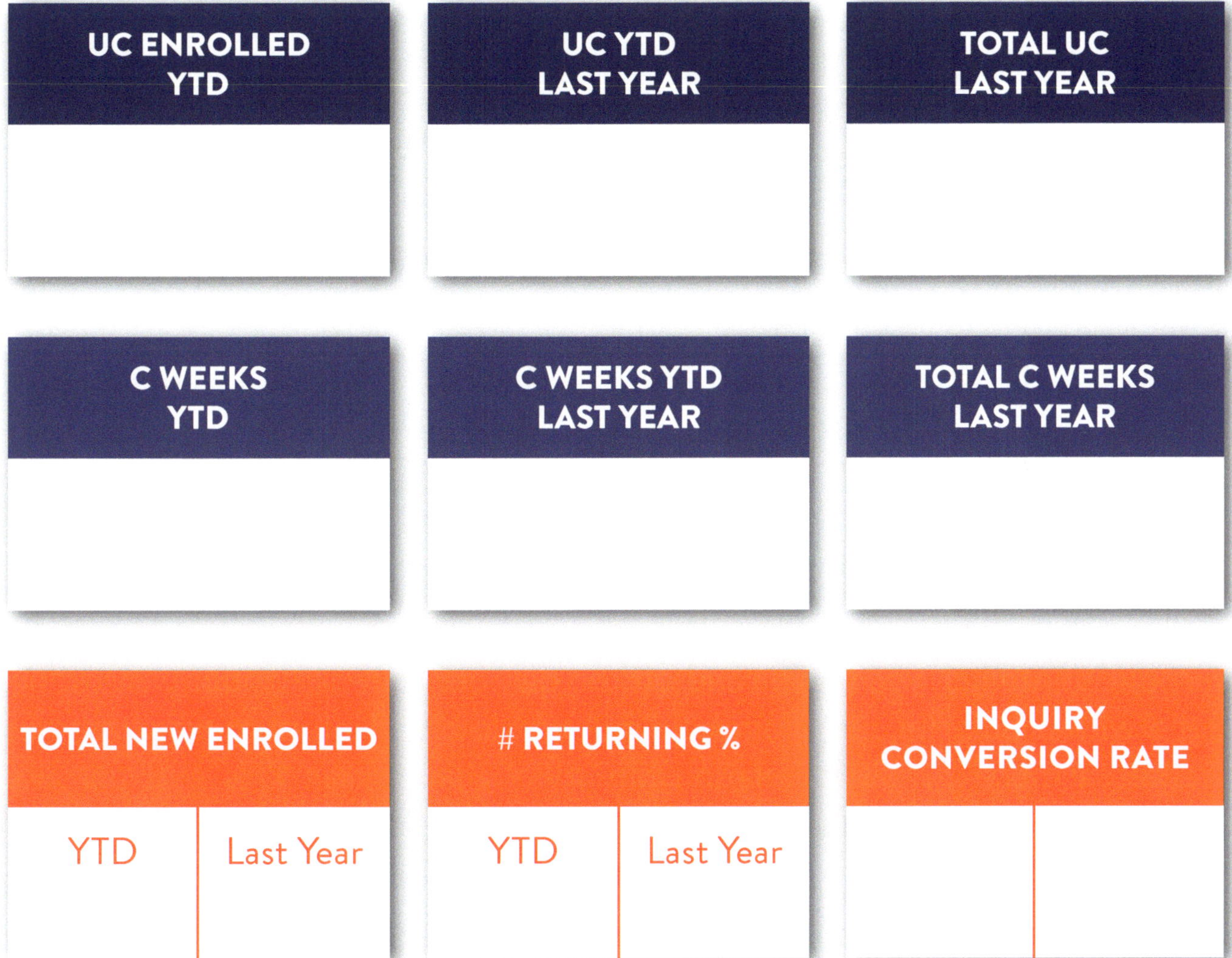

Tracking Statistics enables you to set goals, recognize trends, and proactively respond.

UC = Unique Campers / number of individual campers enrolled at a specific time - e.g., 43 campers were registered on January 20 for a total of 43 unique campers

C WEEKS = Camper Weeks / number of weeks booked at a specific time - e.g., 43 campers were registered for two weeks each on January 20 for a total of 86 camper weeks

Inquiry Conversion Rate = number of families who inquire about your programs compared to the number who register for your camp

YTD = Year to Date | **NYE** = Not Yet Enrolled

Thanksgiving is the perfect time for campers to tell their friends and family how much they love camp.

You can help orchestrate this by providing **a link to your most fun and singable camp song** along with the words so campers can teach it after Thanksgiving dinner, record the epic event, and then post it to YouTube for all to see. It would also be fun for campers to have a short, exciting camp video available to show everyone at some point during the celebration.

Parents have told me that they and the camper's grandparents especially appreciate 'the gift of Camp' for the holidays because they don't want to waste money on throw-away gifts.

If your camp hosts groups, you must make the time to **share what you do for kids** in a short but intriguing and powerful presentation every time visitors are on site. It's worth the effort to spread the word about camp!

Yes, once enrolled, you could send off the Camper/Parent Handbooks and be done with it but, ongoing 'handholding,' a little bit of information at a time, creates a more 'attentive relationship style' that makes kids and parents feel more comfortable about the upcoming event AND strengthens 1st-year retention numbers.

In the 'Make It Happen' Section (next page), two items are critical. Check your automated responses to confirm that they are current. Too often left unattended, they can be embarrassing. Please respond immediately to ALL parent inquiries and questions.

Stay aware of your enrollment tracking and, if you see negative trends, take action immediately!

NYE* PREVIOUS CAMPERS

- **Challenge Campers In a Fun Way to Teach Their Family a Camp Song at Thanksgiving and Post a Video to YouTube**

**NYE = Not Yet Enrolled*

NYE* PREVIOUS PARENTS

- **Offer an Option to 'Give the Gift of Camp' for the Holidays**
- Send a 'Secret' Favorite Camp Dessert Recipe to Make to Surprise Camper for Thanksgiving

NEW ACQUISITIONS

- **Confirm that ALL Facility User Groups Know About Your Camp Programs and, When Possible, Follow Up with Individual Promotions**
- Promote Camp to Membership, Volunteers, Board, Friends & Families

NEXT SUMMER'S CAMPERS

NEW
- 3rd Installment of 'Getting to Know About Camp'

RETURNING
- **In a Fun Way, Challenge Campers to Teach Their Family a Camp Song at Thanksgiving and Post a Video to YouTube**

NEXT SUMMER'S PARENTS

NEW
- 3rd Installment of Prepping for Camp

RETURNING
- **Send a 'Secret' Favorite Camp Dessert Recipe to Make to Surprise Camper for Thanksgiving**

ALL
- **Offer Camp Swag as Holiday Gifts**
- Director Blog/ Trust Building Media Post

Make It Happen

Confirm Post-Registration Automated Follow-up

Leverage Parental Attitudes that Kids Need Camp Today

Utilize Powerful Messages & Resonating Visuals

All Communication Honors Your Personal and Camp **Brands**

Respond Immediately!

Scrutinize Retention and Enrollment Details

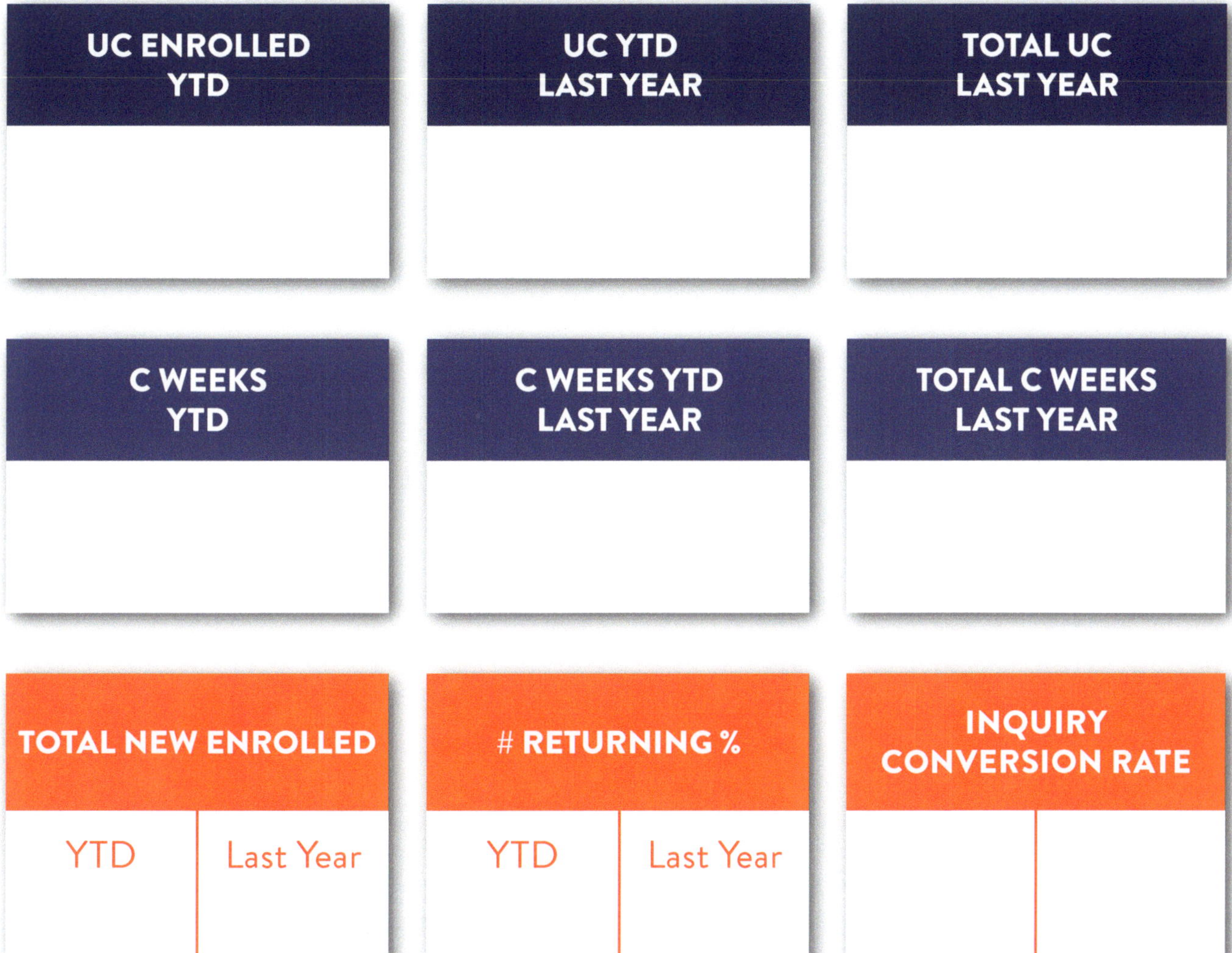

Tracking Statistics enables you to set goals, recognize trends, and proactively respond.

UC = Unique Campers / number of individual campers enrolled at a specific time - e.g., 43 campers were registered on January 20 for a total of 43 unique campers

C WEEKS = Camper Weeks / number of weeks booked at a specific time - e.g., 43 campers were registered for two weeks each on January 20 for a total of 86 camper weeks

Inquiry Conversion Rate = number of families who inquire about your programs compared to the number who register for your camp

YTD = Year to Date | **NYE** = Not Yet Enrolled

December is the ideal month to Reconnect and Plan for Outreach to Increase New Acquisitions.

It's natural to **send Holiday or New Year's Messages** to Last Year's Campers, Previous Campers who could still return in the same role, Campers who could now be staff, Campers who are now parents, Campers who are grandparents and Campers who are likely donors. The messaging of the good work that the camp is doing for kids is the same but their potential connection point is what changes according to the group so that each individual knows that they are being spoken to personally.

As you are determining which **advertising, camp fairs, and community events** are most likely to be successful for you, compare your parent profile with the demographics of those who view the ads or attend the festivities.

Over the years, campers and counselors have confirmed at not-for-profit and private camps that Attendance Awards are meaningful to them, especially if all respect the ceremony that accompanies that ritual.

It is tempting to rely on Social Network postings to convey critical information for camp families; however, the percentage of the population you reach is minimal. If information is important, it should be emailed or texted for 100% saturation, although there are no guarantees how many will read what is sent.

Consistently in Focus Groups, parents who have kids in camps that always have wait lists report that the most appreciated characteristic is that 'the camp always takes or returns my calls right away!' Think about it.

NYE* PREVIOUS CAMPERS

- ☐ **Use Short Staff Videos to Rekindle Emotional Connections**
- ☐ Send Generic Holiday/New Year Cards or Personal Messages to Different Groups
- ☐ Remind Campers of Attendance Awards, and, If You Don't Have Them, Create Them Now

NYE = Not Yet Enrolled

NYE* PREVIOUS PARENTS

- ☐ **Use Resources like http://thankstocamp.org to Remind Parents why Camp is Critical**
- ☐ Summarize Social Network Postings that Parents May Have Missed and Email to All
- ☐ Send a Family Holiday or New Year Card

NEW ACQUISITIONS

- ☐ **Leverage Opportunities to Connect with Large Numbers of New Families via Camp Fairs, Advertising, Geographic Area Saturation, Membership, Community Connections, Schools, New Community Developments**

NEXT SUMMER'S CAMPERS

NEW
- ☐ **4th Installment of 'Getting to Know About Camp'**
- ☐ Holiday/New Year Card

RETURNING
- ☐ **Send Generic Holiday/New Year Cards or Personal Messages to Different Groups**
- ☐ Use Short Staff Videos to Rekindle Emotional Connections

NEXT SUMMER'S PARENTS

NEW
- ☐ **4th Installment of Prepping for Camp or a Dr. Deborah Gilboa or Dr. Tina Payne Bryson Article/video**

ALL
- ☐ **'Thank You for Trusting Us With Your Child' Holiday Greeting**
- ☐ Camper Referral System Reminder
- ☐ Director Blog/Trust Building Media Post

Make It Happen

Always Be Accessible and Responsive

Present Your Camp Confidently and Evocatively

Avoid 'Buyer's Remorse' By Staying Connected with New Campers & Parents After Their Registration

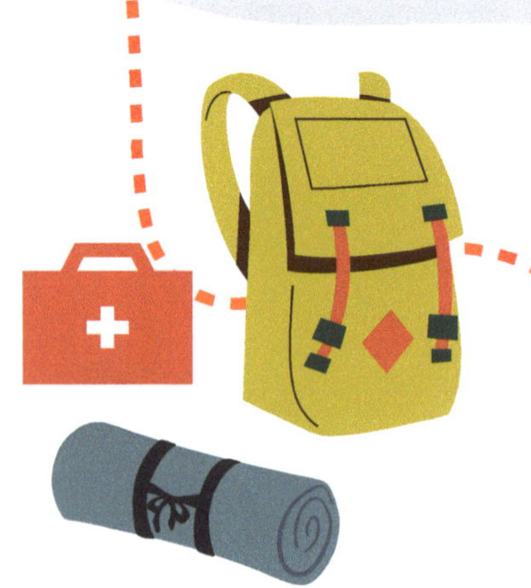

Continue to Focus on a 'Noticeably Improved Product'!

Scrutinize Retention and Enrollment Details

STATISTICS

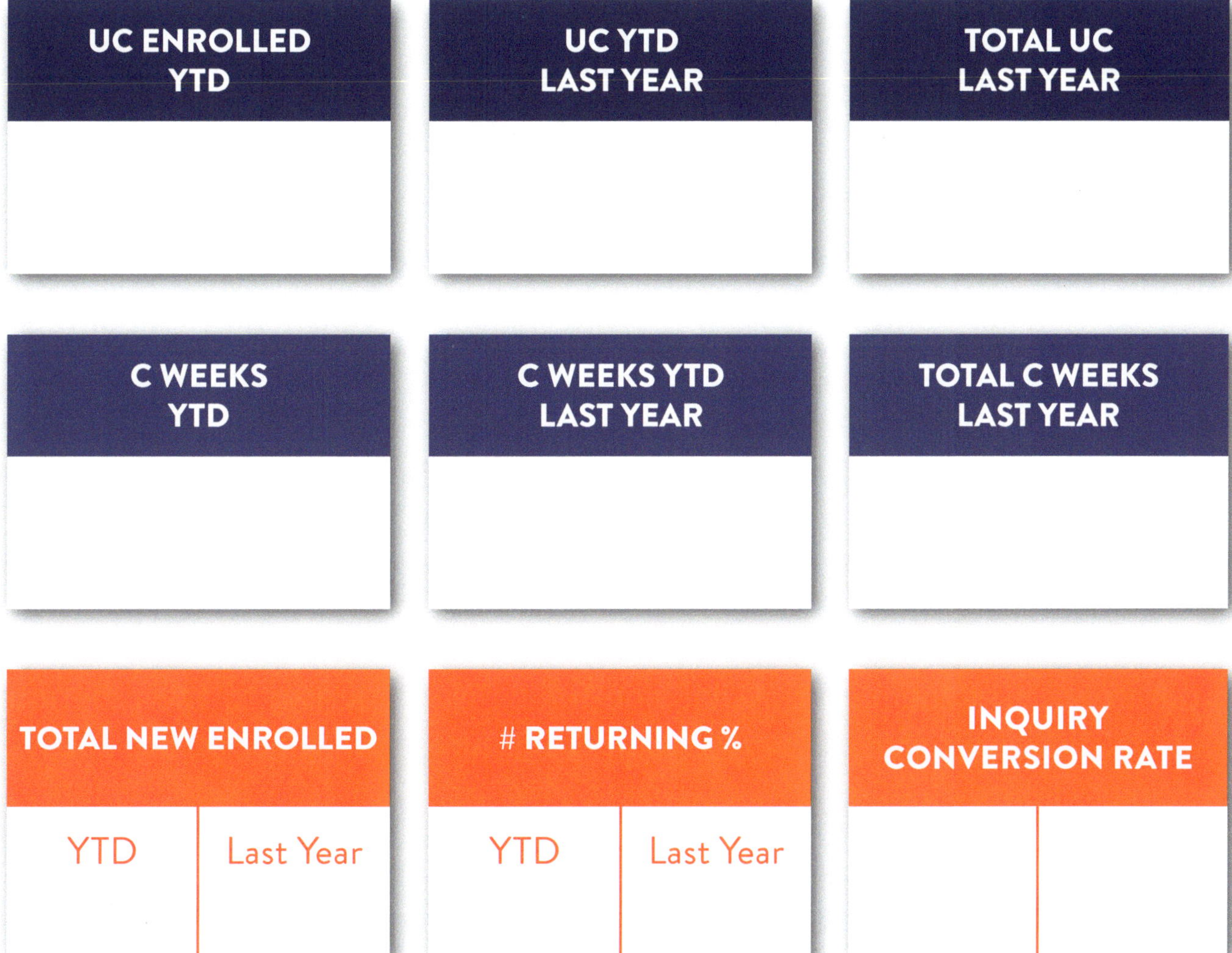

Tracking Statistics enables you to set goals, recognize trends, and proactively respond.

UC = Unique Campers / number of individual campers enrolled at a specific time - e.g., 43 campers were registered on January 20 for a total of 43 unique campers

C WEEKS = Camper Weeks / number of weeks booked at a specific time - e.g., 43 campers were registered for two weeks each on January 20 for a total of 86 camper weeks

Inquiry Conversion Rate = number of families who inquire about your programs compared to the number who register for your camp

YTD = Year to Date | **NYE** = Not Yet Enrolled

Resolve Now to Stay On Top of Your Intentional Marketing Game Plan!

It's all about making **a consistent effort**, even a little bit every day, to get into a rhythm so that everything you do is manageable. Your marketing efforts become as routine as what happens every weekday when your alarm goes off, and you get ready for work.

Each new inquiry is taken care of in a way that ensures the family sees your camp as special, that you nurture relationships with those who are already enrolled to make sure they do not have second thoughts, and you naturally re-connect those not registered to the camp experience so they decide to return. All this is happening while you are proactively creating opportunities to meet families who are likely to appreciate and purchase the life-impacting camp experience you provide for today's kids.

Returning campers and parents appreciate knowing their survey input makes a difference. Let them know what fine-tuning is happening to the program and logistics as a result of survey results to assure them that you are always seeking to improve.

And please don't underestimate the power of **creating a 'Knock Their Socks Off' short email message** that describes your camp experience. Ask all Friends of your Camp to share it with those who have children with 'This is where my child goes to camp,' in the subject line.

Camp marketing is easy if you consistently follow a routine. And when you do, you'll achieve your enrollment goals!

NYE* PREVIOUS CAMPERS

- ☐ **'Come Back' and 'What's New' Promo**

**NYE = Not Yet Enrolled*

NYE* PREVIOUS PARENTS

- ☐ **Encourage Immediate Enrollment to Secure Session of Choice**
- ☐ Improvements Planned for Next Summer as a result of Survey Input
- ☐ Finalize Social Media Plan

NEW ACQUISITIONS

- ☐ **Feature How Kids Need Camp**
- ☐ Cut & Paste 'Crafted' Message From Friends of Camp To Their Networks
- ☐ Confirm Inquiry Courtship & Follow Up Language
- ☐ Leverage Potential through Camp Fairs/Alumni, Board/Membership, and Schools/Communities

NEXT SUMMER'S CAMPERS

- ☐ **Countdown to Camp with Jargon/Traditions for New Kids**
- ☐ Give Returners Progressive Responsibilities
- ☐ Differentiate New from Returning Camper Conversations for Maximum Impact.

NEXT SUMMER'S PARENTS

- ☐ **Target Conversations with New & Returning Parents Who Have Different Expectations**
- ☐ Create Anticipation
- ☐ Reinforce a Culture of Referrals with an Incentive System
- ☐ Director Blog/Trust Building Media Post

Make It Happen

Distinguish Yourself in All Areas

Claim Your "Handle" on All Social Networks

Promote Your Communication Plan & Access To You

Ask 'The Closing Question' – 'Is Our Camp a Good Fit For Your Child?'

ReACT to Trends

Scrutinize Retention and Enrollment Details

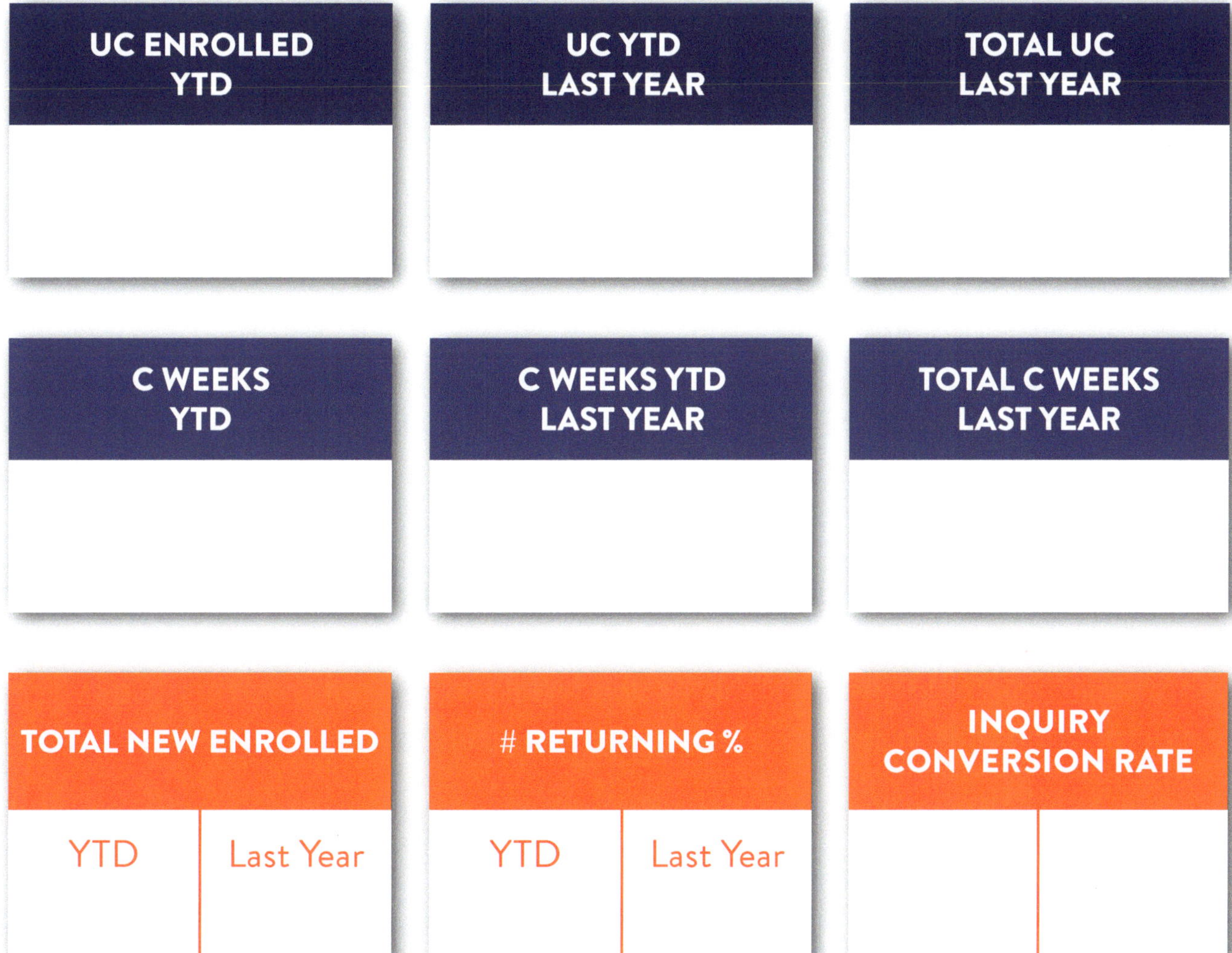

Tracking Statistics enables you to set goals, recognize trends, and proactively respond.

UC = Unique Campers / number of individual campers enrolled at a specific time - e.g., 43 campers were registered on January 20 for a total of 43 unique campers

C WEEKS = Camper Weeks / number of weeks booked at a specific time - e.g., 43 campers were registered for two weeks each on January 20 for a total of 86 camper weeks

Inquiry Conversion Rate = number of families who inquire about your programs compared to the number who register for your camp

YTD = Year to Date | **NYE** = Not Yet Enrolled

Celebrate Valentine's Day, which should be 'I LOVE CAMP DAY'!

It's the perfect opportunity to get not yet enrolled former campers to reconnect with camp and the returning and new campers to get excited about the upcoming summer. It is also an emotionally effective deadline for the next enrollment incentive.

February also allows you to counter the trend that inquiring parents have shared consistently in Focus Groups... that most of the camps they initially contact NEVER get back to them and SELDOM follow up. Once you have an inquiry, it is like a gold nugget and it is up to you to follow up regularly to cultivate their interest and trust.

In the MAKE IT HAPPEN Section this month, a familiar phrase appears. Commit to a 'Noticeably Improved Product' which will happen if you tackle logistical issues now. Since no camp is perfect, **address those problems from last summer** that kept things from going as smoothly as you would have liked, whether they were the details of meals, transportation, or communications.

And while you're at it, make sure that your Enthusiast who love camp and are likely to refer potential campers and staff to you have all the promotional tools^Q they need to do their jobs easily and well.

Regarding the last entry in the MAKE IT HAPPEN Section, if you have not already done so, run group session lists from last year, highlight campers who enrolled for the upcoming summer, and then study those who still need to register. **Connect immediately with the 'OMG!' families you knew would return but haven't registered yet.** Familiarize yourself with the unit/bunk mix before the call to determine likely issues so that you have solutions ready when you speak to the parents.

Keep at it! Better to do one or two promotional items well than attempt multiple elements you can't sustain.

NYE* PREVIOUS CAMPERS

- **Encourage Campers to Post a Camp Pic or Retell a Favorite Camp Story by Feb 14 (I Love Camp Day) to Create Nostalgia for Camp With a Camp Store Prize**
- Send an I ♥ Camp Card, Video or Counselor Communication

**NYE = Not Yet Enrolled*

NYE* PREVIOUS PARENTS

- **Make Scripted Phone Calls To Cause Sign Ups Followed by Email with Link to Enroll**
- Return on Investment Promo to Help Parents Understand Benefits of Camp
- Raffle incentive for all enrolled by Feb 14 (I Love Camp Day) to encourage momentum

NEW ACQUISITIONS

- **Know Your CLV - Camper Lifetime Value - To Make Smart Marketing Decisions**
- Remind Inquiries of the Benefits of Camp
- Inquiry Follow-up
- Connect through Open Houses, Parlor Meetings, Community Venues, and Virtual Forums

NEXT SUMMER'S CAMPERS

- **'Your 1st Day' Comic or Coloring Book for New Campers**
- I ♥ Camp Card, Video or Counselor Communication for All
- Create Nostalgia for Camp With a Camp Store Prize

NEXT SUMMER'S PARENTS

- **Advise All Parents of Communication Strategy During Camp**
- New Parent Insights
- Parent Handbook with Express Check-in First Day Option[Q]
- 'Who's Important' Web Page - Staff Bios & Pics as Hired
- Referral Promotions

Make It Happen

Commit to a 'Noticeably Improved Product'

Tackle Logistical Glitches in Marketing and Operations

Replenish Promotional Tools for Camper & Staff Applicant Ambassadors

Personalize the Data, See Who is Not Yet Enrolled & Take Action

ReACT to Trends

Scrutinize Retention and Enrollment Details

STATISTICS

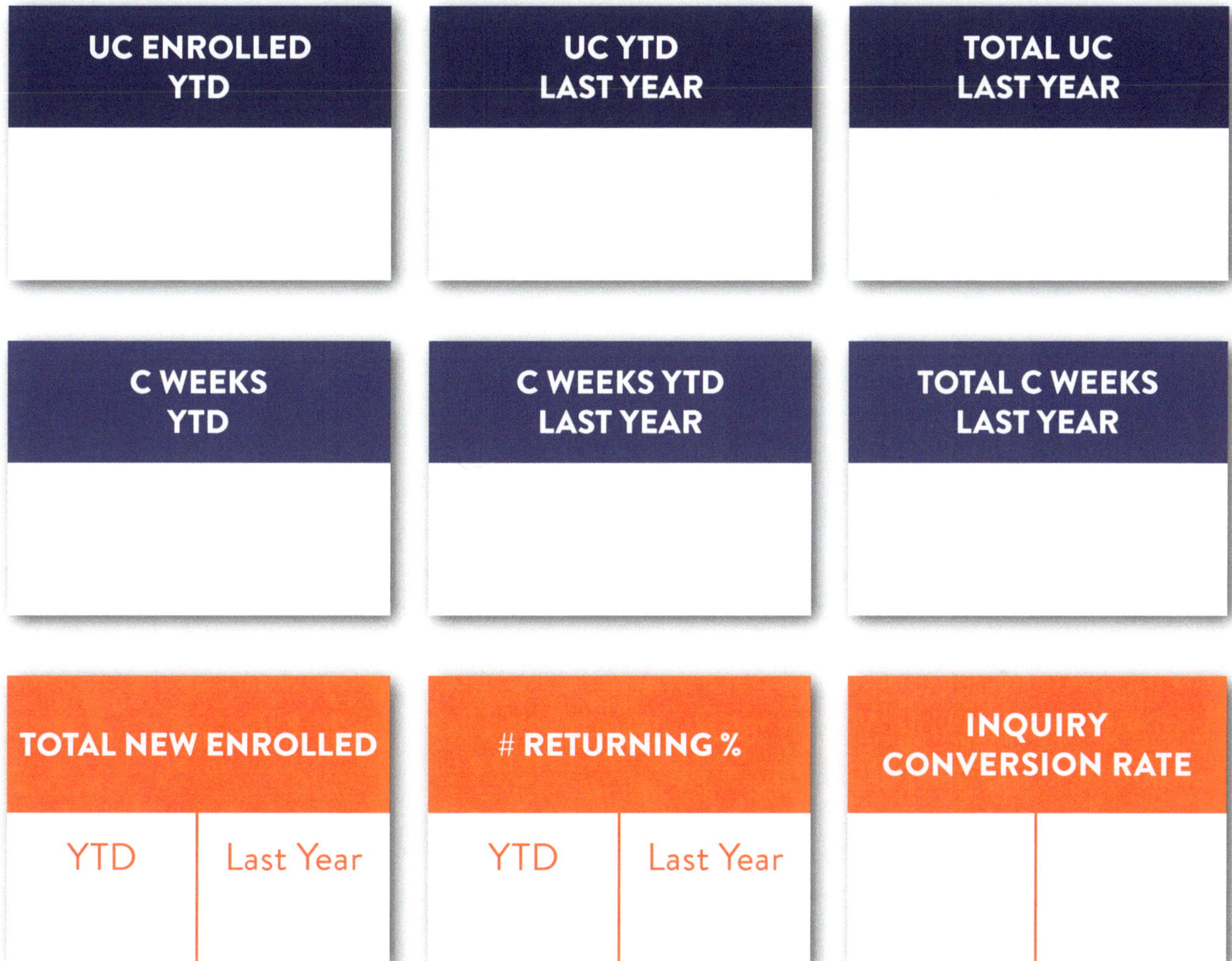

Tracking Statistics enables you to set goals, recognize trends, and proactively respond.

UC = Unique Campers / number of individual campers enrolled at a specific time - e.g., 43 campers were registered on January 20 for a total of 43 unique campers

C WEEKS = Camper Weeks / number of weeks booked at a specific time - e.g., 43 campers were registered for two weeks each on January 20 for a total of 86 camper weeks

Inquiry Conversion Rate = number of families who inquire about your programs compared to the number who register for your camp

YTD = Year to Date | **NYE** = Not Yet Enrolled

Whenever a parent asks about a timeline to register, encourage an immediate response because 'you don't want them to miss out'.

Reminder... when a parent enrolls their child, please make sure the confirmation of the registration, session, and payment is sent immediately in a professionally playful and warm manner that **sets the stage for your ongoing communications**. Also, confirm that the new camper receives a 'we're so glad you're going to be with us this summer' message (possibly via the parent's email) that is appropriate to their age group. **These two initial contacts establish the style for your ongoing relationship with them and your subsequent year's retention.**

Parents and campers love to become familiar with the staff who will be with you during the upcoming summer. And it's easy to keep them informed if you assemble your 'Staff Gallery' as individuals are hired. An appropriate pic and a short bio submitted as part of the hiring process provide the necessary elements to keep your Web Page updated. **Send families the link at least once a month between now and summer.**

As you begin Camp Tours, 'dress' your facility. In March, April and May, even the best facility without campers, laughter, and bright colors is boring. Secure great pics of the waterfront, the challenge course, the tennis, and the dance pavilion. Blow them up as large as they can be and laminate them. Place them strategically for all to see as they approach the venue. **Increase the 'WOW!' factor and get more sales.**

And finally, most importantly, **plan now for your method of Quality Control this summer**. Many camps use the 'OMG!' Forms very successfully. ●——————————➤

NYE* PREVIOUS CAMPERS

- ☐ **Introduce Returning & New Counselors**
- ☐ Emotional Connectors To Special Places, Events or Rituals

**NYE = Not Yet Enrolled*

NYE* PREVIOUS PARENTS

- ☐ **Registration Promos Right After Spring Vacations End**
- ☐ **Return on Investment (ROI)** Conversations Help Parents Make Decisions To Enroll
- ☐ Understand which Campers are Registered and from which Bunks/Units to be Prepared to Address any Repeat Family Concerns

NEW ACQUISITIONS

- ☐ **Camp Tours on 'Dressed' Facility With Pics & Videos**
- ☐ Follow Up With All Inquiries/School User Groups/Alums/ Community Contacts
- ☐ Study Analytics to Learn How New Clients Found You
- ☐ Sense of Urgency - 'Enroll As Soon As You Can So You Don't Miss Out'

NEXT SUMMER'S CAMPERS

NEW
- ☐ **Introduce Returning & New Counselors**
- ☐ Intro To Camp Culture & Rituals
- ☐ Build Confidence With Camp Culture Knowledge

RETURNING
- ☐ **Introduce Returning & New Counselors**
- ☐ Strengthen Connections & Responsibility to Camp Community

NEXT SUMMER'S PARENTS

NEW
- ☐ **Introduce Returning & New Counselors**
- ☐ Affirm Decision to Enroll with Effective and Warm Communications

ALL
- ☐ **Introduce Returning & New Counselors**
- ☐ Resolve Client Issues Immediately
- ☐ Director Blog/Trust Building Media Post

Make It Happen

Plan for Quality Control

Focus on Engagement, Rituals, Orientation, and Activity Execution

Increase Survey Responses By Showing Changes Made Because of Parent & Camper Input

Create a Culture of Innovation

ReACT to Trends

Scrutinize Retention and Enrollment Details

STATISTICS

UC ENROLLED YTD	UC YTD LAST YEAR	TOTAL UC LAST YEAR

C WEEKS YTD	C WEEKS YTD LAST YEAR	TOTAL C WEEKS LAST YEAR

TOTAL NEW ENROLLED		# RETURNING %		INQUIRY CONVERSION RATE	
YTD	Last Year	YTD	Last Year		

Tracking Statistics enables you to set goals, recognize trends, and proactively respond.

UC = Unique Campers / number of individual campers enrolled at a specific time - e.g., 43 campers were registered on January 20 for a total of 43 unique campers

C WEEKS = Camper Weeks / number of weeks booked at a specific time - e.g., 43 campers were registered for two weeks each on January 20 for a total of 86 camper weeks

Inquiry Conversion Rate = number of families who inquire about your programs compared to the number who register for your camp

YTD = Year to Date | **NYE** = Not Yet Enrolled

As the countdown to camp starts in April, there are three critical areas...

Recruiting More Campers

You can do so from previously enrolled registrants and new inquiries. Three of the four Strategic Communications (Section #2 of the next page) for NYE Parents can also be used very effectively with new inquiries and as follow-up for those who inquired previously.

'Why Kids Need Camp Today' is a particularly persuasive post-pandemic argument since benefits are much more appreciated now, and the new 'stuff' you've invested in indicates a fresh approach that resonates with consumers.

Preparing New Campers & Their Parents for Opening Day and Beyond

The more groups know about the upcoming summer, the better. They will be nervous but they'll be confident that they can handle everything because you've been intentional about preparing them. And when you do a good job, your efforts will be rewarded with increased retention rates!

Partnering with New & Returning Parents

You have a unique opportunity to develop relationships that will bring kids back year after year. On an ongoing basis, share your opinions and resources from folks like Drs. Deborah Gilboa & Tina Bryson. Here are samples parents appreciate. ●➞

Finally, in April, **refine your Survey Tools for on-site Camper Assessments and ratings of the Parent Experience** to be sent out immediately after the session. This will help you identify areas to improve, not just what you are doing well. But please don't waste your time doing this work if it is not your intention to tabulate the results immediately and take action to fine-tune your product.

NYE* PREVIOUS CAMPERS

- ☐ **Promote What's New This Year, Video and/or Memories of Camp Video with Message from Popular Returning Counselors**
- ☐ Run an Interactive Online Contest/Game with Participants Getting Gift Certificates to Camp Store

NYE = Not Yet Enrolled

NYE* PREVIOUS PARENTS

- ☐ **4 Strategic, Brief & Powerful Communications...**
  1. **Why Kids Need Camp Today**
  2. **Reinvest in Your Camper**
  3. **Benefits for Your Camper**
  4. **New 'Stuff' This Summer**

NEW ACQUISITIONS

- ☐ **Work with Schools, Clubs & Community Partners To Find Potential Campers**
- ☐ Pinterest Shows Your Expertise in Families and Appeals to Decision-Makers (See Examples at QR Code link)
- ☐ Video Ads to Reach Millennial Parents
- ☐ Present at Community Events
- ☐ Follow-up All Inquires!

NEXT SUMMER'S CAMPERS

NEW
- ☐ **Create an Interactive Video Map of Camp to Establish Camper Confidence**

ALL
- ☐ **Ask Campers, 'What Do You Want to Accomplish This Summer?'**
- ☐ Interactive Online Contest/Game with Participants Getting Gift Certificates to Camp Store

NEXT SUMMER'S PARENTS

NEW
- ☐ **Present Webinar for New Parents to Establish Comfort and Familiarity**

ALL
- ☐ **Announce Changes Via Webinar**
- ☐ Send Link to Parenting Blog Article
- ☐ Director Blog/Trust Building Media Post

Make It Happen

Update Internal & Parental Crisis Communication Plans

Onboard Staff to Achieve Culture Immersion

Plan to Capture Marketing Resources (photos, videos, testimonials, promos)

Finalize Survey Tools to Secure Quality Input from Campers, Parents, & Staff

Track Tour Conversions

Scrutinize Retention and Enrollment Details

STATISTICS

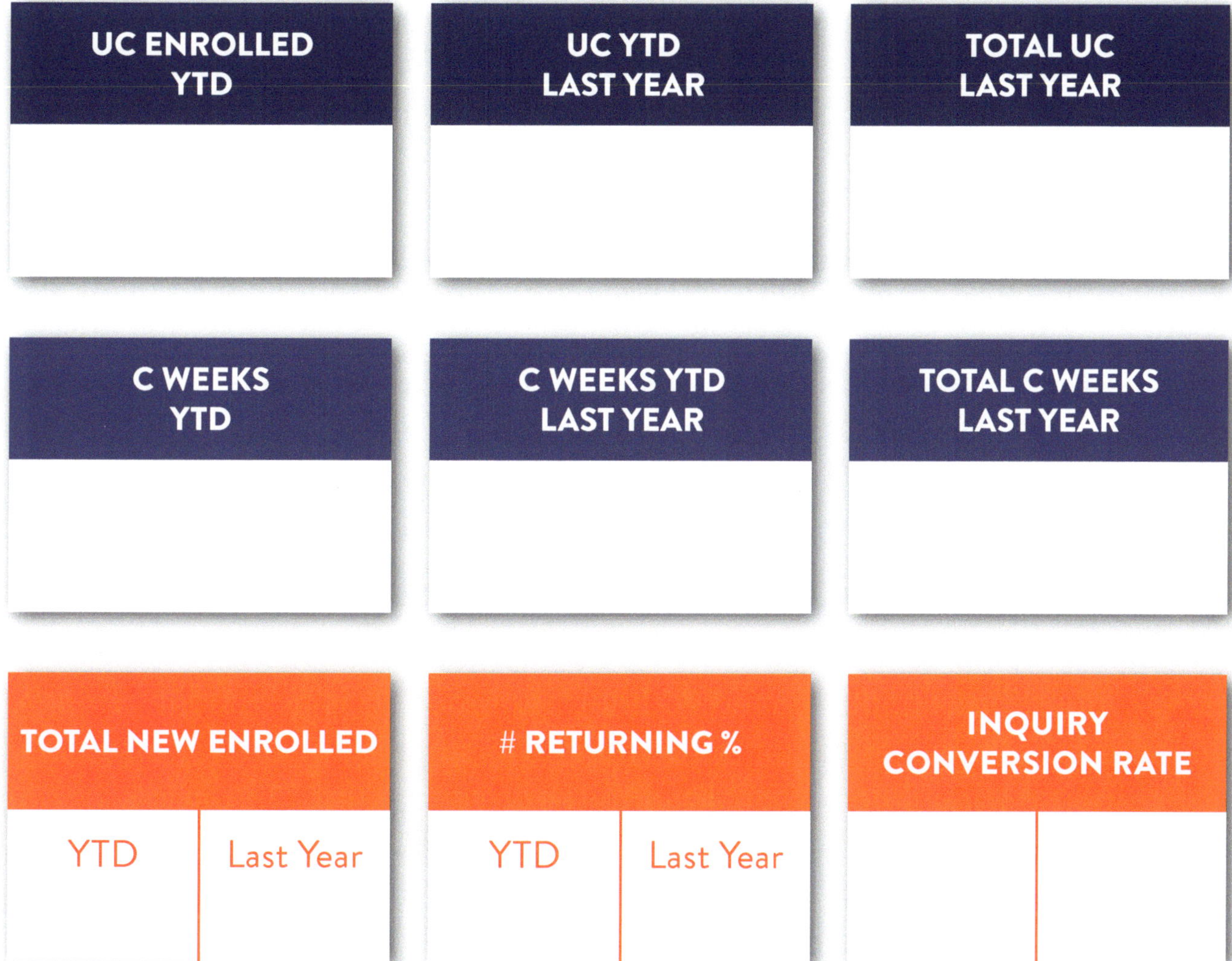

Tracking Statistics enables you to set goals, recognize trends, and proactively respond.

UC = Unique Campers / number of individual campers enrolled at a specific time - e.g., 43 campers were registered on January 20 for a total of 43 unique campers

C WEEKS = Camper Weeks / number of weeks booked at a specific time - e.g., 43 campers were registered for two weeks each on January 20 for a total of 86 camper weeks

Inquiry Conversion Rate = number of families who inquire about your programs compared to the number who register for your camp

YTD = Year to Date　　|　　**NYE** = Not Yet Enrolled

Yes, you're busy in May, but a little extra effort can bring in more campers and make a difference in retention.

For Not Yet Enrolled Campers, a CUTE **communication about missing them at camp** sent via snail mail or their parent's email, in combination with a question to their parents about 'what is a better alternative to camp?', could make a difference.

In addition to inviting all inquiries to visit camp during the summer, encourage alumni and friends of camp to visit. **Plan your tours at times that show camp at its best,** select an optimal tour route, determine key talking points, prepare responses to frequently asked questions, and train gregarious guides to deliver tours that will 'knock their socks off'. When visitors stop by, determine how and when they were affiliated with the camp and confirm their contact information.

All staff and tour guides must be trained to answer the 'How big is your camp?' question confidently and without hesitation. It is not about acreage, or the total number of campers served in the summer or during a session. The response should be personalized to the parent asking: 'In David's group, there will be 11 other boys his age and 3 counselors.' Then, if asked, the other numbers can be shared.

It's critical that you check daily for parents who abandon their online registration carts and do not finish signing up. Call immediately to determine how you can help. Whether it's a technical glitch or a family issue, **you don't want them distracted from enrolling their child for camp**.

And finally, to provide the best Camper and Parent Experiences possible, empower and encourage all staff that when they see something wrong or even a little off, they should say something. The more aware everyone is, the better your camp product will be!

NYE* PREVIOUS CAMPERS

- ☐ **Send a 'Camp Won't Be The Same Without You' Promo** Knowing Some Parents May Not Appreciate This

**NYE = Not Yet Enrolled*

NYE* PREVIOUS PARENTS

- ☐ **'What's A Better Alternative to Camp?' Final Promo**
- ☐ Staff Bios with Schools They Attend
- ☐ Reach Out To Parents with a Personal 'Ask': Use Their Name and Child's Name in a Video Shot at Camp if Possible

NEW ACQUISITIONS

- ☐ **Invitation to 'See Camp in Action' with Pre and Post-Visit Communications**
- ☐ Stats-Motivated Final Outreach to Fill Specific Sessions
- ☐ Implement Daily Cart Abandonment Strategy to Get Parents to Finish Registration

NEXT SUMMER'S CAMPERS

NEW

- ☐ **Ongoing Prep for First Timers**

RETURNERS

- ☐ **Remind Returning Campers that Each Has a Responsibility to Make New Campers Feel Welcome in the Community**

NEXT SUMMER'S PARENTS

NEW

- ☐ **New Parent Webinars To Explain Complicated Parts of Sending Kids to Camp**
- ☐ On-going Assurance of 'Wise Decision to Select Your Camp'

ALL

- ☐ **Another Parenting Blog from Dr. Deborah Gilboa or Dr. Tina Payne Bryson Article**
- ☐ Director Blog/Trust Building Media Post

Make It Happen

Implement a Quality Control System

Deliver 'Knock Their Socks Off' Tours

Ask the 'Tough Question' Confidently – 'Is our camp a good match for your child?'

Empower Counselors to Say Something if They See Something Questionable About Program Quality

Acknowledge Data Realities

Scrutinize Retention and Enrollment Details

STATISTICS

UC ENROLLED YTD	UC YTD LAST YEAR	TOTAL UC LAST YEAR

C WEEKS YTD	C WEEKS YTD LAST YEAR	TOTAL C WEEKS LAST YEAR

TOTAL NEW ENROLLED		# RETURNING %		INQUIRY CONVERSION RATE	
YTD	Last Year	YTD	Last Year		

Tracking Statistics enables you to set goals, recognize trends, and proactively respond.

UC = Unique Campers / number of individual campers enrolled at a specific time - e.g., 43 campers were registered on January 20 for a total of 43 unique campers

C WEEKS = Camper Weeks / number of weeks booked at a specific time - e.g., 43 campers were registered for two weeks each on January 20 for a total of 86 camper weeks

Inquiry Conversion Rate = number of families who inquire about your programs compared to the number who register for your camp

YTD = Year to Date | **NYE** = Not Yet Enrolled

During June, July, and August, while camp is in session, your marketing efforts need to be on automatic.

You simply do not have the time or energy while camp is in session to tend to promotional details. **Everything needs to be in place before the summer so that marketing continues without you even thinking about it.** During camp… you must be responsive and accessible to parents, provide ample communication, and be certain that each camper's issue is addressed immediately and resolved.

Tours, and **you must allow folks to see camp in action**, need to show your camp at its best with guides who are engaging and committed to the philosophy. The pre-tour conversations and follow-up must be warm and timely to maximize interest and sales.

Most important, in staff training, please address '==The Moment of Truth=='. Imagine two campers walking down a path at camp with a favorite counselor. Their laughter and conversation are interrupted when one camper looks trustingly at the counselor and inquires, 'You'll be here next year, right?' and without hesitation, the counselor shoots back, 'Nope, goin' to grad school'.

You know what just happened. Those campers are definitely not returning. Now we're not encouraging lying but we are asking you to help your counselors see how influential they are and substitute a more reasonable response like, 'I love camp so much, I want to come back every year. What about you?' FYI… Camps all over the country now teach this technique in their training, and they report that it has made a difference.

Finally, it is to your advantage to do **Parent Surveys within 48 hours** after each session rather than waiting until the end of the summer so that you can fix issues as the summer progresses. **Now, go for it!**

CURRENT CAMPERS

- ❑ **Pre-Departure, Have Kids Identify Proudest Camp Moments, What They Accomplished, & What They Want to Achieve Next Year at Camp**
- ❑ Have Arriving Campers Identify & Note Personal Goals
- ❑ Arrange For Groups to Get a Glimpse of Next Year's Program
- ❑ On-Site Surveys, Tabulation, Action

CURRENT PARENTS

- ❑ **Promote Extensions or Returns During the Summer**
- ❑ Post Pictures & Hype Hashtag **#yourcamp20??**
- ❑ Provide Child's Experience Details
- ❑ Respond Immediately to Parent Concerns
- ❑ Thank Parents for Trust & Encourage ID of Camper Changes[Q]
- ❑ Parent Surveys 48 Hours After Each Session

NEW ACQUISITIONS

- ❑ **Train Tour Guides with Route & Language**
- ❑ Invite All Inquiries, Alums & Friends to 'See Camp in Action'
- ❑ Have Visitors Meet Director & Leadership During 'Best Times'
- ❑ Use Pre & Post-Visit Communications to Maximize Impact

NEXT SUMMER'S CAMPERS

- ❑ **Revitalize Birthday at Camp Tradition to Maximize Impact Throughout the Year**
- ❑ Confirm that the Program is Progressive (Campers Can Access More Programs As They Age) to Ensure High Retention

NEXT SUMMER'S PARENTS

- ❑ **Publish Rates & Dates for Next Year Before the Summer Starts**
- ❑ Commence Next Season's Registration During Summer if Possible to Leverage Established Emotional Connections
- ❑ Director Blog and Trust Building Media Posts

Make It Happen

Teach Counselors How to Respond When Asked... 'Are You Coming Back Next Year?'

Role Model & Encourage Engagement to Establish a Culture of Belonging

Utilize a 'Quality Control' Protocol Like the 'OMG!' Form to Fine-Tune Your Camp Experience

Tabulate Survey Results as Collected & React To Improve Product Quality

AND NOW, IT'S UP TO YOU!

Just having the Playbook in your possession is not enough. You've got to **do the work consistently each month**, be creative, and be resourceful. When you see an opportunity, you need to capitalize on it. And when you believe you're absolutely going in the right direction, you've got to stay the course and not waiver. Most critically, when you realize that it's going to take more effort than you expected to be successful, you must push forward.

The camp marketplace is extraordinarily competitive and you must always strive for excellence… to deliver Camper and Parent Experiences that are meaningful and memorable. This way, you have a convincing marketing message to share with returning and prospective families as you recruit throughout the year.

The fun part of camp is the summer. The tedious, difficult, demanding work comes with recruiting campers and staff during the other three seasons.

But You Are Not Alone! You have the Playbook to guide you and we are only an email away. So don't hesitate to be in touch…

Travis Allison, Co-Founder/Co-Owner
Go Camp Pro
travis@gocamp.pro
gocamp.pro

Joanna Warren Smith, President
Camp Consulting Services
campconsulting@charter.net
camp-consulting.com

PLAYBOOK MARKETING DICTIONARY

Alumni: Those who have attended your camp are your most significant and productive resources if you maintain connections with them. The most likely to return as campers are those who were with you the previous year or two, while more distant participants could return as staff, eventually send their children, be active alumni, refer staff/campers, and, ultimately, become donors. 'Alumni' can refer to former campers, staff, parents, and volunteers.

Branding: This term references the values, mission, colors, and symbols that drive a camp's philosophy and are apparent in its marketing content.

CAC (Cost of Acquisition of Camper): It is good business to add up all the costs associated with acquiring new campers, including staff time, and divide it by the number of campers acquired in a specific time frame to determine how much was spent acquiring each new camper and if it was worth it. Knowing the CAC and the Camper Lifetime Value (CLV) can help camps make the most profitable and smart marketing decisions.

Camper Referral System: This intentional business practice encourages and rewards your camp community for proactively promoting your program throughout the recruitment year. This technique is key to increasing the easily acquired word-of-mouth registrations. This practice is becoming more critical in a marketplace crowded with children's summer opportunities.

Camper Weeks (C Weeks): This identifies the number of weeks booked on a specific date and is often compared with that same date in the previous season to identify success or weakness in recruiting methods.

Cart Abandonment Strategy: It is absolutely crucial to immediately reach out to parents who initiate the camp registration process but do not finish.

CLV (Camper Lifetime Value): This term refers to how much money a camp will earn over the years one camper attends. It is determined by multiplying the average number of sessions a camper registers for in a year and multiplying that number by the average number of years children and teens come to your camp.

Content: This refers to the creating, publishing, and distributing of information via email, social media, blog posts, online videos, infographics, or podcasts targeted to a specific group of families.

Conversion: This happens when a consumer purchases a product. In the camp world, this references families who inquire about your programs and then register for your camp.

Focus Groups: These in-person and virtual meetings can be run by an objective facilitator to secure parents' opinions about the camps their children attend.

Hashtags (# symbol+word): On social media, hashtags categorize the content being posted. Use specific hashtags like the camp's name or unique activities to better reach families with those interests.

Inquiry to Conversion Rate: This references the percentage of interested new parents who become sales in a given recruitment year. Tracking the number of inquiries and the actual number of conversions helps determine the impact of follow-up in terms of timing, number of in-person and written communications, and the content of what is being shared.

Marketing Context: Customers are looking for marketing messaging that speaks to their own individual family needs and wants at specific times in their lives.

Market Persona: It's an excellent technique to imagine an ideal parent and camper to represent the characteristics of your target market with names, ages, location, financial background, family, interests, and goals, and then use that characterization as you communicate with your prospective audience. The more detail you utilize, the more personal your marketing messages feel and the more significant impact you have in creating more interest and sales.

Marketing Mix: This references the product, price, place, and promotion used to guide objectives when marketing to the target group.

Metrics: These are the critical numbers associated with a company's marketing performance. This could be the number of leads you get from a specific marketing project, the number of clicks on a link, the number of visitors to a website, and more.

Moment of Truth: The critical instant when a camper inquires of a beloved counselor if they will be returning next summer, and the staff member thoughtlessly responds, 'No, going to grad school!' or when trained, responds in such a way that the camper is eager to return.

New Acquisitions: These are families, with similar attributes to your current clients who have no connection to you and have the potential to become buyers of your camp product.

Not Yet Enrolled (NYE): Former campers and their parents who are not currently enrolled for the next season. They should be the number one focus of each recruitment season.

Organic Reach: This indicates the number of views a social media post receives through unpaid means... shares, likes, comments, and word of mouth.

Program Context: These are intentional efforts to establish a picture of what will happen and what a child has experienced or help parents fully understand what their children are doing at camp.

Retention: This critical attribute refers to campers who return because of what you do during the summer to ensure that the Camper Experience is engaging and progressive and, equally important, what you do during the school year to keep the camper and the parent connected to camp.

ROI (Return on Investment): This evaluates the profitability of an investment by subtracting the sales growth from the marketing cost and then dividing it by the marketing cost. So, if sales for your camp increase by $1,000 after you spend $100 on advertising a new ropes course, then your Marketing ROI is 900%. Additionally, parents have referenced their ROI regarding the benefits for their children as a result of the tuition they paid for camp.

SEO (Search Engine Optimization): Through SEO, the goal is to increase the placement of your camp's website on the Search Engine Results Page by improving page load times, using inbound and outbound links, having optimized photos, creating quality content, and more.

SERP (Search Engine Results Page): This webpage displays search results for a business or topic when searching on Google, Firefox, Bing, etc.

SWOT Analysis: The intentional process of understanding an operation's Strengths, Weaknesses, Opportunities, and Threats is essential. With leadership input, it helps build on what is being done well, determines what is lacking, and develops plans for how to minimize risks.

Target Market/Audience: This is a group of people with shared characteristics that make them representative of ideal camp families. This group should be Measurable, Accessible, Actionable, Distinguishable, and Substantial. Collectively, they should match your current, preferred camper family profile.

Touch Points: This term refers to places where campers and their parents interact with the camp (website, social media, chat, phone calls, events, etc.). Knowing Touch Points helps determine where marketing strategies should be focused.

Unique Campers (UC): This statistic references the number of individual children and teens enrolled as of a given date or for an entire summer. It is helpful in comparing enrollments as the recruitment season is progressing YTD (year to date) to the previous year and the total for the preceding summer.

Value Proposition: This refers to the promise that is made to families when they are buying a camp experience. Ask yourself, 'What transformation happens in kids because of our camp program?' and then market that benefit confidently.

Travis Allison, *Co-founder*
Go Camp Pro

travis@gocamp.pro | gocamp.pro

Travis hates mushy fruit but loves jam.

It's not just fruit that Travis thinks about in great detail. His creative and conscientious persona has made him a keynote speaker at conferences across the US and Canada.

Travis is an award-winning Camp Professional who is the Executive Producer of the seven Go Camp Pro podcasts. He created the world's largest online Facebook Group for Camp Pros and has helped clients bring hundreds of campers to great camps worldwide. Search **TED.com** for his TEDx talk about how his camp counselor changed the course of his life.

Travis believes it's his job to inspire summer camp leaders worldwide to be **so GREAT** that parents realize their children must have a summer camp experience.

Joanna Warren Smith, *President*
Camp Consulting Services

campconsulting@charter.net | camp-consulting.com

Joanna has assessed hundreds of not-for-profit, private, resident and day camps acquiring a unique industry perspective of best business practices. Years of Parent Focus Groups have enabled her to understand their expectations of camp and what motivates families to inquire, purchase and return. Through individualized strategies, Joanna has assisted camp businesses in reaching capacity enrollments and maximizing retention because she's passionate about the positive impact that a quality camp experience should have on today's kids.